A Belated Industry

A Belated Industry

Jane Addams'
Groundbreaking Exposé of
Working Conditions for
Women in Industrial Chicago
(Annotated)

Jane Addams

Cedar Lake Classics

Copyright © 2023 by Cedar Lake Classics

This is a proofread and newly designed edition of a public domain work.

CONTENTS

1 | To the Reader   1

    FOOTNOTES   **21**
ABOUT JANE ADAMS   **23**

1

To the Reader

The industry which the title of this paper designates as belated is that of domestic labor, which is belated, both ethically and industrially; the status of its ethics operating very largely as the determining factor in its industrial situation.

It may be well to make clear at once that this paper does not treat of this occupation as a domestic art, in which the members of the household engage and spend time which would otherwise have no economic value. As an art it is charming and destined to endure so long as women cherish their homes and express affection by personal service. This paper treats of the occupation solely as an industry, by means of which large numbers of women are earning a livelihood. An attempt is made to present this industry from the point of view of those women who are working in households for wages. [1]

This industry was little affected by the industrial revolution of the eighteenth century, and is a surviving remnant of the household system which preceded the factory system. Both employers and employees, for the most part, hold moral conceptions and notions of duty which are tinged with feudalism. There is a tendency for each worker to become isolated from her fellow workers; to be dependent upon the protection and goodwill of her employer, and to have little share in the corporate life of the community. The employees in this industry practically lead the lives of those who have not discovered the power to combine; of those who "cannot create a sufficiently coherent organization to sustain themselves under changing conditions."

We are all more or less familiar with the conditions of the trades affected most quickly by the industrial revolution. If we have not read the reports of the investigations undertaken by the distracted English Parliament, we have at least read the German poems and English stories concerning the misery of the displaced weavers who, upon the application of steam power to weaving, were obliged to leave their hand looms in the country and adjust themselves to the conditions of hastily-built towns. We know that there were painstaking, industrious and virtuous men among the weavers, who were too dull to seize upon the changed conditions of their trades, and who continued to work many hours a day at their hand looms until they and their families perished miserably. The possession of certain individual virtues did not make them of industrial value.

This breaking-up of long established industrial habits and occupations and the necessity for a difficult readjustment comes about constantly with changing conditions, and it is easy to believe that we are in the midst of one of these sweeping industrial changes now; in fact, that it has already come about in regard to many commodities formerly produced in the household which are now produced in factories; that it would naturally come about in regard to most of them, if women did not oppose it and fatuously believe that within these old methods is bound up the sanctity of family life. Most of us can remember the conscientious struggle with which our grandmothers slowly gave up homemade candles, and some of us may dimly recall homespun sheets. All of us know something of the conservative reserve with which our mothers, later, gave up the pleasures and economies of homemade soap in spite of the lively competition and seductive advertisements offered by the factory product.

As industrial conditions have changed, the household has become simplified, from the medieval affair of journeymen, apprentices and maidens who spun and brewed, to the family proper; to those who love each other and live together in ties of affection and consanguinity. Were this process complete, we should have no problem of household employment. But, even in households comparatively humble, there is still one alien, one who is neither loved nor loving. The modern family has dropped the man who made its shoes, the woman who spun its clothes, and to a large extent the woman who washes them, but it stoutly refuses to drop the woman who cooks its food; it strangely insists that to do that would be to destroy family life. The cook is uncomfortable, the family is uncomfortable; but it will not drop her as all her fellow-workers have been dropped, although the cook herself insists upon it. So far has this insistence gone that every possible concession is made to retain her. I know an employer in one of the suburbs who built a bay at the back of her house so that her cook might have a pleasant room in which to sleep, and one in which to receive her friends. This employer naturally felt aggrieved when the cook refused to stay in her bay. Viewed in an historic light, this employer might just as well have added a bay to her house for her shoemaker, and then deemed him ungrateful because he declined to live in it.

The employer misunderstood the situation. She did not realize that the desire to live with one's kinsfolk is stronger in most of us than the desire for the comforts to be found in a bay. The household employee has no regular opportunity for meeting other workers of her trade, and of attaining with them the dignity of a corporate body. The industrial isolation of the household employee results, as isolation in a trade must always result, in a lack of progress in the methods and products of that trade and a lack of aspiration and education in the workman. Whether we recognize this isolation as a cause or not, I think we are all ready to acknowledge that household labor has been in some way belated; that the improvements there have not kept up with the improvement in other occupations. It is said that the last revolution in the processes of cooking was brought about by Count Rumford, who died a hundred years ago. This is largely due to lack of esprit de corps among the employees, which keeps them collectively from fresh achievements, as the absence of education in the individual keeps her from improving her implements. [end page 538]

Under this isolation, not only must one set of utensils

serve divers purposes, and as a consequence tend to a lessened volume, and lower quality of work, but inasmuch as the appliances are not made to perform the fullest work, there is an amount of capital invested disproportionate to the result when measured by the achievement in other branches of industry. More important than this is the result of the isolation upon the worker herself. There is nothing more devastating to the inventive faculty, nor fatal to a flow of mind and spirit, than the constant feeling of loneliness and the absence of that fellowship which makes our public opinion.

If an angry foreman reprimands a girl for breaking a machine, twenty other girls hear him, and the culprit knows perfectly well their opinion as to the justice or injustice of her situation. In either case she bears it better for knowing that, and for not thinking it over in solitude. If a household employee breaks a utensil or a piece of porcelain and is reprimanded by her employer, too often the invisible jury is the family of the latter, who naturally uphold her censorious position and intensify the feeling of loneliness in the employee.

The isolation of the household employee is perhaps inevitable so long as the employer holds her belated ethics; but the situation is made even more difficult by the character and capacity of the girls who enter this industry. In any great industrial change the workmen who are permanently displaced are those who are too dull to seize upon changed conditions. The workmen who have knowledge and insight, and who are in touch with their time, quickly reorganize. There are many noble exceptions, but it follows that on the whole the enterprising girls of the community go into factories, and the less enterprising go into households. It is not a question of skill, of energy, of conscientious work, which will enable a girl to rise industrially while she is in the household; she is not in the rising movement. She is belated in a class composed of the unprogressive elements of the community, and which is recruited constantly from the victims of misfortune and incompetence, by girls who are learning the language, girls who are timid and slow, or girls who look at life solely from the savings bank point of view. The distracted housekeeper struggles with these unprogressive girls, holding to them not even the well-defined and independent relation of employer and employed, but the hazy and constantly changing one of mistress to servant. A listener attentive to a conversation between two employers of household labor, and we certainly all have opportunity to hear such conversations, would often discover a tone implying that the employer was abused and put upon; that she was struggling with it solely because she was thus serving her family and performing her social duties; that otherwise it would be a great relief to her to throw up the whole thing and "never have a servant in her house again." Did she follow this impulse she would simply yield to the trend of her times, and accept the system of factory production. She would be in line with the industrial organization of her age. Were she in line ethically, she would have to believe that the sacredness and beauty of family life do not consist in the processes of the separate preparation of food, but in sharing the corporate life of the community, and in making the family the unit of that life.

The selfishness of a modern mistress, who, in her narrow

A BELATED INDUSTRY

social ethics, insists that those who minister to the comforts of her family, shall minister to it alone, that they shall not only be celibate, but shall be cut off more or less from their natural social ties, excludes the best working people from her service. A man of dignity and ability is quite willing to come into a house to tune a piano. Another man of mechanical skill will come to put up window shades. Another of less skill, but perfect independence, will come to clean and lay a carpet. These men would all resent the situation and consider it quite impossible if it implied the giving up of their family and social ties, and living under the roof of the household requiring their services. Most of the cooking and serving and cleaning of a household could be done by women living outside and coming into a house as a skilled workmen does, having no "personal [end page 540] service" relation to the employer. There is no reason why the woman who cleans windows in a house, should not live as full a domestic and social life as the man who cleans windows in an office. If the "servant" attitude were once eliminated from household industry, and the well-established one of employer and employee substituted, the first step would be taken toward overcoming many difficulties.

Although this household industry survives in the midst of the factory system, it must, of course, constantly compete with it. To all untrained women seeking employment--save those with little children or invalids depending upon them, to whom both factory and household labor are impossible, and who are practically confined to the sewing trades--a choice is open between these two forms of labor.

There are few women so dull that they cannot paste labels on a box, or do some form of factory work, few so dull that some perplexed housekeeper will not receive them at least for a trial into her household. Household labor then has to compete constantly with factory labor, and women seeking employment, more or less consciously compare these two forms of labor in point of hours, in point of permanency of employment, in point of wages and in point of the advantage afforded for family and social life. Three points are easily disposed of: (1) In regard to hours there is no doubt that the factory has the advantage. The average factory hours are from seven in the morning to six in the evening, with the chance of working overtime in busy seasons. This leaves most of the evenings and Sundays entirely free. The average hours of household labor are from six in the morning until eight at night, with little difference in seasons. There is one afternoon a week, with an occasional evening, but Sunday is almost never wholly free. (2) In regard to permanency of position the advantage is found clearly on the side of the household employee, if she proves in any measure satisfactory to her employer, for she encounters much less competition. (3) In point of wages the household is again fairly ahead, if we consider not the money received but the opportunity offered for saving money. This is greater among household employees because they do not pay board, the clothing required is simpler, and the temptation to spend money in recreation is less frequent.

The minimum wages paid an adult in household labor may be fairly put at two dollars and a half a week; the maximum at six dollars, this excluding the comparatively rare opportunities

A BELATED INDUSTRY

for women to cook at forty dollars a month, and the housekeeper's position at fifty dollars a month. The factory wages, viewed from the savings bank standpoint, may be smaller in the average, but this I believe to be counterbalanced in the minds of the employees by the greater chance which the factory offers for increased wages. A girl over sixteen seldom works in a factory for less than four dollars a week, and she always cherishes the hope of at last being a forewoman with a permanent salary of fifteen or twenty-five dollars a week. Whether she attains this or not, she runs a fair chance of earning ten dollars a week as a skilled worker. A girl finds it easier to be content with four dollars a week, when she pays for board, in a scale of wages rising towards ten dollars, than to be content with four dollars a week and pay no board in a scale of wages rising towards six dollars, and the girl well knows that there are scores of forewomen at sixty dollars a month for one forty-dollar cook or fifty-dollar housekeeper. In many cases this position is well taken economically for, although the opportunity for saving may be better for the employees in the household than in the factory, her family saves more when she works in a factory and lives with them. The rent is no more when she is at home. The two dollars and fifty cents a week which she pays into the family fund more than covers the cost of her actual food, and at night she can often contribute towards the family labor by helping her mother wash and sew. This brings us easily to the fourth point of comparison, that of the possibilities afforded for family life. It is well to remember that women, as a rule, are devoted to their families; that they want to live with their parents, their brothers and sisters and kinsfolk, and will sacrifice a good deal to accomplish this. This devotion is so universal that it is impossible to ignore it when we consider women as employees.

Young unmarried women are not detached from family claims and requirement as young men are, and, so far as my observation goes, are more ready and steady in their response to the needs of the aged parents and helpless members of the family. But women performing labor in households find peculiar difficulties in the way of enjoying family life, and are more or less dependent upon their employers for possibilities to see their relatives and friends. Curiously enough the same devotion to family life and quick response to its claims on the part of the employer, operates against the girl in household labor and places her in a unique position of isolation. The employer of household labor, in her zeal to preserve her family life intact and free from intrusion, acts inconsistently and grants to her cook, for instance, but once or twice a week such opportunity for untrammelled association with her relatives as the employer's family claims constantly. This devotion to the narrow conception of family life the men of the family also share. The New York gentleman who lunches at Delmonico's eats food cooked by a chef with a salary of five thousand dollars a year, and prepared with all modern appliances. He comes home hungry and with a tantalizing memory of his lunch to a dinner cooked by a woman with a salary of forty dollars a month, with only those appliances possible in a small kitchen. The contrast between the lunch and dinner is great, but the aforesaid gentleman quiets his discontent by his reflection, that, in eating a dinner cooked under his own roof, he is in some occult manner contributing to the sanctity of family life; though his business mind knows full well that, in actual money, he is paying more for his badly cooked dinner than for his well-cooked lunch; that in submitting to such conditions he is failing to use the powers of organization and combination which have made his business so successful. The household employee, in addition to her industrial isolation, is also isolated socially.

It is well to remember that the household employees, for the better quarters of the city and suburbs, are largely drawn from the poorer quarters, which are nothing if not gregarious. The girl is born and reared in a tenement house full of children. She goes to school with them, and there she learns to march, to read and write in companionship with forty others. When she is old enough to go to parties, those she attends are usually held in a public hall and are crowded with dancers. If she works in a factory, she walks home with many other girls, in much the same spirit as she formerly walked in school with them. She mingles with the young men she knows, in frank economic and social equality. Until she marries she remains at home with no special break or change in her family and social life. If she is employed in a household, this is not true. Suddenly all the conditions of her life are changed. This change may be wholesome for her, but it is not easy, and the thought of the savings bank does not cheer one much, when one is twenty. She is isolated from the people with whom she has been reared, with whom she has gone to school, and among whom she expects to live when she marries. She is naturally lonely and constrained away from them, and the "new girl" often seems "queer" to her employer's family. She does not care to mingle socially with the people in whose house she is employed, as the girl in the country when she "works for" a country neighbor often does, and she suffers horribly from loneliness. This wholesome instinctive dread of social isolation is so strong that, as every city intelligence office can testify, the filling of situations is easier or more difficult just in proportion as the place offers more or less companionship. Thus, the easy situation to fill is always the city house with five or six employees, shading off into the more difficult suburban home with two, and the utterly impossible lonely country house.

There are suburban employers of household labor who make heroic efforts to supply domestic and social life to their employees, who take the domestic employee to drive, arrange to have her invited out occasionally, who supply her with books and papers and companionship. Nothing could be more praiseworthy in motive, but it is seldom successful in actual operation. In the first place it is a forced relationship, and nothing in the world can be worse than a simulacrum of companionship. The employee may have a genuine friendship for her employer and a pleasure in her companionship, or she may not, and the unnaturalness of the situation comes from the insistence that she has, merely because of the propinquity. I should consider myself an unpardonable snob if, because a woman did my cooking, I should not hold myself ready to have her for my best friend, to drive, to read, to attend receptions with her, but that friendship might or might not come about, according to her nature and mine, just as it might or might not come about between me and my college colleague. On the other hand, I should consider myself very stupid if merely because a woman cooked my food and lived in my house I should insist upon having a friendship with her, whether her nature and mine responded to it or not. It would be folly to force the companionship of myself or my family upon her when doubtless she would vastly prefer the companionship of her own friends and her own family.

The unnaturalness of the situation is brought about by the fact that she is practically debarred by distance and lack of leisure from her own natural ties, and then her employer feeling sorry, insists upon filling the vacancy in interests and affections by her own tastes and friendship. She may or may not succeed, but the employee should not be thus dependent upon the good will of her employer. That in itself is feudal. Added to all this is a social distinction which the household employee feels keenly against her, and in favor of the factory girls, in the minds of the young men of her acquaintance. A woman who has worked in households for twenty years told me that when she was a young and pretty nurse girl, the only young men who "paid her attention" were coachmen and unskilled laborers. The skill in the trades of her suitors increased as her position in the household increased in dignity. When she was a housekeeper, forty years old, skilled mechanics appeared, one of whom she married. Women seeking employment understand perfectly well this feeling, quite unjustifiable I am willing to admit, among mechanics, and it acts as a strong inducement towards factory labor. I have long ceased to apologize for the views and opinions of working people. I am quite sure that on the whole they are just about as wise and just about as foolish as the views and opinions of other people, but that this particularly foolish opinion of young mechanics is widely shared by the employing class can be easily demonstrated. The contrast is further accentuated by the better social position of the factory girl, and the advantages provided for her in the way of lunch clubs, social clubs, and vacation homes, from which girls performing household labor are practically excluded by their hours of work, their geographical situation, and a curious feeling that they are not as interesting as factory girls. It is not the object of this paper to suggest remedies ; but if the premise in regard to the isolation of the household employee is well taken, and if the position can be sustained that this isolation proves the determining factor in the situation, then certainly an effort should be made to remedy this, at least in its domestic and social aspects. To allow household employees to live with their own families and among their own friends, as factory employees now do, would be to relegate more production to industrial centers administered on the factory system, and to secure shorter hours for that which remains to be done in the household. It might be possible that the employer of household labor would have to go back, at least during the period of transition, to the original office of "lady," that of "bread giving" to her household. It might be necessary for her to receive the prepared food and drink and serve it herself to her family and guests, but truly that is no hardship, which may be made a grace and a token, and there is no reason why in time the necessary serving at a table should not be done by a trained

A BELATED INDUSTRY

corps of women as fine as the Swiss men who make the table d'hote of the European hotel such a marvel of celerity.

In the fewer cases in which the household employees have no family ties, doubtless a remedy against social isolation would be the formation of residence clubs, at least in the suburbs, where the isolation is most keenly felt. Indeed the beginnings of these clubs are already seen in the servants' quarters at the summer hotels. In these residence clubs the household employee could have the independent life which only one's abiding place can afford. This, of course, presupposes a higher grade of ability than household employees at present possess ; on the other hand it is only by offering such possibilities that the higher grades of intelligence can be secured for household employment. As the plan of separate clubs for household employees will probably come first in the suburbs, where the difficulty of securing and holding "servants " under the present system is most keenly felt, so the plan of buying cooked food from an outside kitchen and of having more and more of the household product relegated to the factory will probably come from the comparatively poor people in the city, who feel most keenly the pressure of the present system. They already consume a much larger proportion of canned goods and baker's wares and "prepared meats" than the more prosperous people do, [2] because they cannot command the skill nor the time for the more tedious preparation of the raw material. It is comparatively easy for an employer to manage her household industry with a cook, a laundress, a waitress, etc.

The difficulties really begin when the family income is so small that but one person can be employed in the household for all these varied functions, and the difficulties increase and grow almost insurmountable as they fall altogether upon the mother of the family, who is living in a flat, or worse still, in a tenement house, where one stove and one set of utensils must be put to all sorts of uses, fit or unfit, making the living room of the family a horror in summer,, and perfectly insupportable in rainy washing days in winter. Such a woman is living in a complicated age, totally without the differentiation of functions and utensils which that age demands. A fuller social and domestic life among household employees would be the first step toward securing their entrance into the larger industrial organizations by which the needs of a community are most successfully administered. Many a girl who complains of loneliness, and who relinquishes her situation with that as her sole excuse, feebly tries to formulate her sense of restraint and social maladjustment. She sometimes says that she "feels so unnatural all the time." [3] And when she leaves her employer her reasons are often incoherent and totally incomprehensible to that good lady, who naturally concludes that she wishes to get away from the work and back to her dances and giddy life, content to stand many hours in an unsanitary factory, if she has these.

The charge of the employer is only a half truth. These dances may be the only organized form of social life which the disheartened employee is able to mention; but she has felt the social trend of her times, and is trying to say what an old English poet said five centuries ago: "Forsooth, brothers, fellowship is heaven, and lack of fellowship is hell; fellowship is life and lack of fellowship is death; and the deeds that ye do upon earth, it is for fellowship's sake that ye do them." Two other contemporary industries are similar in condition and situation to that of domestic labor. The workers in these two industries are also isolated. The worker in the first is the woman who endeavors to support herself "by taking in sewing." She is the last unit of the sweating system-the home finisher. The majority of her sisters in all the other trades have gone into the factories, she alone remains at home and turns her already uncomfortable tenement into a workshop. Isolated as the sewing woman is, industrially she still has advantages over the household employee, in that she may remain in the same part of town with her kinsfolk and her natural social associations. In that respect she is nearer the conditions of factory life. Indeed, there is a detectable tendency to absorb her into the factory, a tendency hastened by the sweating investigations, workshop acts, the trades unions slowly being formed among sewing women, and one might add by the conscience more slowly still being evolved amongst the consumers in regard to clothing manufactured in tenement houses. These causes all operate toward the establishment of factories. [4]

Farming is another unorganized industry depending upon isolated workers, which is not in the least holding its own in our industrial development. There are doubtless many causes to explain the increase of cities, and the steady depopulation of the country. In a careful estimate, however, it should not be ignored that the farmer relies more and more upon the labor of the few people living upon his farm. The gathering together of all the neighbors for hay-making and house-raising, the apple-paring parties, and the corn-husking bees are all experiences of the past. These mixed the pleasures of social intercourse with the labor of production, and implied the vicinage in their very conception. Much discussion has of late been expended on the discontent of the farmer. It has been discovered that while one-half of the entire population of the United States is agricultural, in the last two decades this one-half of the population have amassed but one-tenth of the wealth of the country. This failure to amass their share of wealth, in spite of their almost incessant exertions, doubtless arises chiefly from the lack of association and cooperation among farmers, from the diffusion rather than the concentration of their energies.

To quote from a recent writer, in the Forum, "Not only does a lack of organized effort among farmers result in much misdirected energy and consequent economic loss, but it works an even more serious injury by placing the farmer population at a disadvantage in the great industrial contest in which other and coordinated industries--by virtue of their ability for thorough concentration and organization--have a superior advantage. The American farmer has not yet mastered the problem of combined action, consequently he has not fully "realized" upon his energies. The economic loss, however, great as it is, is but a trifle, compared with the woeful waste. of social energy. From this comes that abiding soul weariness suffered by so many farmers, and still more by their wives and their children. This, again, reacts against their economic value." If the farmer is doomed to have a poorer social life than men in other vocations, then the bright farmer's boys, naturally craving those things which sweeten and brighten human life, will not stay upon the farm, and the force which drives them into their share of associated life is just as natural and just as much to be counted upon as the force which drives the wind through the tree tops.

If the girl who engages in domestic labor is doomed to a narrow social life, if she is isolated from her family and natural industrial associations, then it follows that the brightest girl will not engage in domestic labor, but will follow the natural trend of their times, towards factory work and associated effort. The cry of the whip-poor-will never struck so lonely upon the heart of the young man sitting in the dusk upon the farmhouse porch as it did last summer, because the farm work itself and the farmhouse production has never been so far away from the spirit and tendency of its times. All over the country various experiments are being made to reorganize the conditions of farm life, that the farmers may live in villages, where may be sustained some of the higher forms of education and social civilization. Will women again fail in this time of reorganization, as they utterly failed to reorganize their half of the world's work, upon the introduction of the factory system? Will they utterly disregard the lonely girl within their household, and when she demands a fuller life, and leaves that household, will they weakly continue to complain, rather than make a vigorous effort for bringing household industry into the trend of the times? To fail to apprehend the tendency of one's age, and to fail to adapt the conditions of an industry to it is to leave that industry ill adjusted and belated.

JANE ADDAMS

JANE ADDAMS
HULL-HOUSE

FOOTNOTES

1. The opinions in it have been largely gained through experiences in a Woman's Labor Bureau, and through conversations held there with women returning from the " situations," which they had voluntarily relinquished in Chicago households of all grades. These same women seldom gave up a place in a factory, although many of the factory situations involved long hours and hard work.

2. The writer has seen a tenement house mother pass by a basket of green peas at the door of a local grocery store, to purchase a tin of canned peas, because they could be easily prepared for supper and " the children liked the tinny taste."

3. The writer has known the voice of a girl to change so much during three weeks of "service" that she could not recognize it when the girl returned to the bureau. It alternated between the high falsetto in which a shy child " speaks a piece," and the husky gulp with which the globus hystericus is swallowed. The alertness and

bonhomie of the voice of the tenement-house child had totally disappeared.

4. he industrial and ethical situation of the sewing woman has been so fully discussed in "Hull-House Maps and Papers" that it is needless to repeat it here serve the home?

ABOUT JANE ADAMS

Childhood and Education

Jane Addams was born on September 6, 1860, in Cedarville, Illinois. She was the eighth child of John and Sarah Addams. Her father, John, was a wealthy miller and local political leader who served as a state senator and supported Abraham Lincoln. Her mother Sarah was a homemaker and very active in the community.

Jane had a privileged but lonely upbringing as a child. She was born with a congenital spinal defect that caused her lifelong health problems. This prevented her from being able to participate in normal childhood activities. She also contracted tuberculosis of the spine at age 4, which caused even more health complications.

As a child, Jane was very bright and ambitious despite her physical limitations. She was well-educated for a girl during that time period. She attended Rockford Female Seminary, one of the best private schools for women in the country. There she became valedictorian of her class and dreamed of attending medical school. However, her plans were interrupted by her recurring health problems.

After graduation, she struggled with depression and

figuring out her purpose in life. She spent time resting, reading, and contemplating how to channel her energy to help others.

Exposure to Poverty

In 1883, at age 23, Jane Addams embarked on an extended tour of Europe with a friend. They visited England, France, Germany, Italy, Greece, and other countries over the next two years. This was a common custom of privileged young women during this time period as a way to gain culture and worldliness.

However, Addams' experience touring Europe exposed her to poverty and human suffering on a level she had never before witnessed. She saw poor children living in crowded, dirty streets and slums. She saw people suffering from disease, injury, and hunger on a daily basis. This was in stark contrast to her relatively comfortable and prosperous upbringing in Illinois.

Addams was profoundly affected by the extreme economic and social disparity she observed between the classes in Europe's major cities. She pondered how society could allow so many people to suffer in poverty. This experience shaped her desire to make meaningful change through social reform.

When Addams returned to the United States in 1885, she dreamed of finding a way to replicate the settlement house model she had seen in England. This model involved university students living in low-income areas to volunteer and elevate their poor neighbors through education and social services. Addams was determined to put her ambition and privilege to use improving the lives of the marginalized and impoverished.

Her first-hand experience observing urban poverty and its effects in Europe ignited Addams' passion for social justice. It inspired her life's work of establishing settlement houses to uplift immigrants and the underprivileged in America's cities.

A Pioneer in Settlement Houses

In 1889, Jane Addams and her college friend Ellen Gates Starr established Hull House in an impoverished immigrant neighborhood in Chicago. Hull House became one of the first settlement houses in the United States.

Addams and other educated, middle-class women moved into the neighborhood and set up programs and services for the community, especially immigrants and children. Hull House provided childcare for working parents, night school classes in English and job skills, clubs for children, legal services, and cultural programs in art and music. The goal was to uplift the immigrant families by providing education, resources and community in an empathetic, neighborly way.

Addams drew on the settlement house model she had seen in England. The concept was to have privileged, educated people volunteer to live in low-income areas in order to share their expertise and resources. The settlement house movement aimed to promote social reform via community engagement and neighborhood revitalization from the inside out.

Addams pioneered putting this concept into action in

America. Hull House was the first large-scale settlement house in the U.S. Soon over 100 settlement houses sprang up in cities across the country, inspired by Addams' example. The movement exposed middle-class Americans to urban poverty and fueled further progressive reforms.

The settlement house movement originated with Addams and Hull House as one of the most hands-on, intimate ways to provide social services. It empowered underprivileged communities, shaped public policy, and transformed urban areas. Addams' vision and leadership paved the way for settlement houses to have an enduring legacy as catalysts for 20th century social reform.

Advocating Social Reform

In addition to pioneering the settlement house movement, Jane Addams was a prominent social reformer and progressive activist on many fronts. She campaigned relentlessly for policy changes to address the underlying problems her settlement houses aimed to alleviate.

Addams advocated for tackling issues such as poverty, child labor, poor sanitation and health conditions, and lack of educational opportunities for the underprivileged. She gave speeches, wrote articles, and lobbied government leaders to try to change laws and social systems.

For example, Addams gave lectures condemning child labor, which was extremely common at the time. She described the awful conditions of children as young as 5 or 6 forced to work long hours in factories. She called for laws prohibiting this exploitation. Addams was also a founding member of the National Child Labor Committee, established in 1904 to further reform efforts.

On the issue of women's right to vote, Addams spoke and campaigned widely in support of women's suffrage. She believed women's perspectives were needed in government to address social welfare concerns. Addams was elected president of the National American Woman Suffrage Association in 1915. She played a key role in lobbying for the 19th amendment granting women's suffrage, which passed in 1920.

In the realm of education, Addams pushed for improving public sanitation and schools in poor areas of Chicago. She also advocated for establishing the first kindergartens and public playgrounds in the city. These efforts helped provide better education and childhood development.

Addams worked tirelessly throughout her life to enact social and political reforms through settlement houses, speeches, coalition building, lobbying, and protesting when necessary. She spearheaded crucial improvements for public health, children, immigrants, women, laborers and more in the early 20th century.

A Leader for Peace

Near the end of World War I, Jane Addams took on a leadership role in the international women's peace movement. She was determined to prevent the horrors she witnessed during the war.

In 1919, Addams presided over the International Congress

of Women meeting in Zurich. This congress established the Women's International League for Peace and Freedom (WILPF), appointing Addams as its first president.

Under Addams' leadership during its early years, the WILPF worked to mediate the conflicts arising from the war and social upheaval. They advocated for peaceful solutions over retributive punishments of Germany and other Central Powers. The WILPF also proposed alternatives to harsh terms within the Treaty of Versailles.

Addams represented the WILPF at the League of Nations foundation conference in 1919. She pushed for the League to address the root socioeconomic causes of war. Although many of the WILPF's proposals were rejected, Addams gave women a voice in shaping the postwar peace process.

From 1919 until her passing in 1935, Addams remained involved in WILPF initiatives such as disarmament campaigns, anti-imperialism efforts, promoting cooperation between former enemies, and providing aid to women and children affected by war.

As the first president of the WILPF, Addams helped establish an enduring international organization for women promoting peace and human rights. Her leadership laid the groundwork for ongoing women's peace movements that carry on her legacy today.

Winning the Nobel Peace Prize

In 1931, at the age of 71, Jane Addams was awarded the Nobel Peace Prize for her pioneering work in social reform

ABOUT JANE ADAMS

and world peace efforts. She shared that year's prize with Nicholas Murray Butler, president of Columbia University.

Addams was recognized by the Nobel Committee specifically for her leadership in founding and developing the settlement house movement. Her groundbreaking work at Hull House serving immigrants and the poor was seen as embodying the ideals of fraternity between peoples and peace through social justice.

The committee also praised Addams' advocacy for women's rights, her support of pacifism, and her leadership in international peace organizations such as the Women's International League for Peace and Freedom. Addams had dedicated her life to addressing the root causes of war and social unrest through social progress and empowerment rather than military force.

In awarding the Nobel Prize to Addams along with an academic leader like Butler, the Nobel Committee aimed to represent both the practical and theoretical efforts needed to achieve peace. Addams' hands-on settlement housework represented the social activism side, while Butler represented the role of universities and intellectuals.

Addams was too ill to travel to accept the award in person, but she expressed her great honor at receiving the prize. As the first American woman to win the Nobel Peace Prize, Addams paved the way for women leaders and reformers to be recognized on the global stage. The award validated her pioneering vision and persistent efforts to create meaningful social change from the ground up.

ABOUT JANE ADAMS

Major Contributions and Legacy

Through Hull House and other settlement houses, Jane Addams pioneered the practice of social work and community engagement in low-income urban neighborhoods. Her programs empowering immigrants, children, and the poor became models for the growing field of social work.

Addams and other settlement workers lived and worked directly in the communities they served. They sought to understand and address root causes of poverty from the ground up. Addams advocated that social work should actively engage marginalized people as partners, not just passive recipients of aid. Her approach valued relationship building as much as skill building.

Addams' social justice advocacy also relied heavily on engaging the community. She strategically used local ethnic clubs, women's groups, unions and other networks to push for reforms and hold politicians accountable.

By the 1920s, Addams' efforts made Hull House one of the largest settlement complexes in the world. Her work influenced later public welfare approaches such as the New Deal programs and Great Society initiatives in the 20th century. It played a major role in establishing social work as a recognized, woman-led profession.

Final Years

Addams worked tirelessly until her last years. She died from cancer on May 21, 1935 in Chicago at the age of 74. She had endured health problems most of her life, but persisted through sheer force of will and passion for her causes.

Addams left an incredible legacy through her pioneering social reform work and activism. She helped transform urban life for immigrants and the poor, while empowering generations of women as leaders and social workers committed to social justice.

www.ingramcontent.com/pod-product-compliance
Lightning Source LLC
Chambersburg PA
CBHW070037040426
42333CB00040B/1709